Other Books by Michael Konik

The Termite Squad
Making It
Becoming Bobby
Reefer Gladness
The Smart Money
Ella in Europe
In Search of Burningbush
Telling Lies and Getting Paid
Nice Shot, Mr. Nicklaus
The Man with the $100,000 Breasts

All Rights Reserved

Published by EggyPress.ca

Edmonton, Alberta, Canada

Cover Design by Simon Trafford

The Termite Squad Cover and Logos by Eric W. Bangle

Photo "Break Something" by Maria Sabrina

"How the Revolution Started" (Bank Guard) was originally published in *Fifth Estate*, Winter 2017.

"No Such Thing" is excerpted from the record album *We Don't Play the Game.* (Feedback Records, 1983).

"Mass Disturbances" is excerpted from *Year 14* (Barrelhouse Books, 2017).

"Five-Sided Story" first appeared in *Caesura: Bronze Edition,* 2017.

"How Money Works" & "My Great Idea" are excerpted from *The Termite Squad* (Eggy Press, 2016).

Konik, Michael

ISBN: 978-0-9959527-1-3

How the Revolution Started

Essays and Impertinent Thoughts

Michael Konik

Eggypress.ca

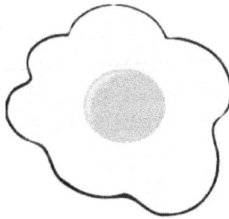

For Lance B. Colak – and all the rest of us gradually awakening.

Contents

"Great!"
My New Satire of America

I've started writing a new book, a broad satire of American Values. Working title: "Great!"

Some will find my portrait of a country gone off the rails a bit dark, the comedy too black, the irony too direct. But in times like these, when a megalomaniac with narcissistic personality disorder doesn't even have to *take* all the power he believes he's entitled to — it's *given* to him by compliant little people who fantasize about one day being as rich and powerful as their hero — satire can't be too broad or too outlandish.

Or have too many plot twists.

Here's my working outline. Our hero is a fellow named Mr. Great. He's a fabulously rich — and, therefore, successful — human being. But like most classical heroes, he has a tragic flaw: Mr. Great is a megalomaniac with narcissistic personality disorder. He's accustomed to taking — *grabbing* might be a better word — what he wants. But when he decides what he wants is to be President of the United States — yes, I know my story is a bit absurd, but give it a chance — the citizenry, or at least a minority of them, form an unlikely coalition of uneducated serfs, highly educated oligarchs, and single-issue conspiracy theorists, and, with the help of an entertainment industry branch known as "the media," deliver the highest office in the land to someone who has been named as a defendant in 163 federal lawsuits.

Good so far?

"Great!" unfolds in the days leading up to Mr. Great assuming the Presidency of the United States. On the day before Mr. Great becomes The Prez, he makes a few declarations, some of them through social media, some through his legion of lackeys, most of them ugly old white men, like their boss. (This part I may have to adjust; in real life, everyone knows how attractive our new administration is.) Mr. Great announces that if it were up to him, he would cut funding for the Department of Justice's Violence Against Women programs.

Mr. Great announces that if it were up to him, he would cut funding for the National Endowment for the Arts. Mr. Great announces that if it were up to him, he would cut funding for the National Endowment for the Humanities. Mr. Great announces that if it were up to him, he would cut funding for the Corporation for Public Broadcasting. The saved money can go toward more important things, like tax breaks for Mr. Great's rich buddies.

Mr. Great announces that if it were up to him, he would cut funding for the Minority Business Development Agency. Mr. Great announces that if it were up to him, he would cut funding for the Economic Development Administration.

Mr. Great announces that if it were up to him, he would cut funding for the Office of Community Oriented Policing Services, because, really, you don't fix something that's already perfect.

Mr. Great announces that if it were up to him, he would cut funding for the Legal Services Corporation. Mr. Great announces that if it were up to him, he would cut funding for the Civil Rights Division of the Department of Justice, because we all agree we need a new nuclear arsenal, not civil rights for all citizens of our nation.

Mr. Great announces that if it were up to him, he would cut funding for the Environmental and Natural Resources Division of the Department of Justice, because we all agree we need more fighter jets, not meddling into the criminal practices of some of America's most admirable job creators in the oil, coal, and precious metals industries.

Mr. Great announces that if it were up to him, he would cut funding for the United Nations Intergovernmental Panel on Climate Change.

Mr. Great announces that if it were up to him, he would cut funding for the Office of Energy Efficiency and Renewable Energy. Mr. Great announces that if it were up to him, he would cut funding for the Office of Fossil Energy.

Then he becomes President.

How the Revolution Started:
Essays and Impertinent Thoughts

On his first day in office, President Great orders the regulatory powers of all federal agencies frozen. Finally, the burdensome meddling ends!

President Great orders the National Parks Service to stop using social media after the Service re-tweets comparative photos of the crowds for the 2009 and 2017 inaugurations. Photos which do not conform to Mr. Great's image of himself.

The next day, President Great brings a claque of 40 cheerleaders to a meeting with the CIA to applaud during a speech that consists almost entirely of attacks on the Press, the one whose reporting does not conform to Mr. Great's image of himself.

President Great's Press Secretary, known affectionately as The Troll, holds a press conference, during which he devotes most of his remarks to attacking the press for accurately reporting the attendance at the inaugural festivities, and says that President Great's inauguration had "the largest audience of any in history, period."

"Great!" I confess, borders on the absurd. But so do some of my other books. Are you diggin' it?

On the second day in office, I ramp up the action, delivering a slew of fascinating plot points woven together in one thrilling narrative of greatness. That's when President Great's White House advisor, affectionately known as Miss Congeniality, defends The Prez's Press Secretary's lies as "alternative facts" on national television. That's when President Great reinstates a global gag order on international organizations that mention abortion as a medical option; doing so results in de-funding.

The next day, with the masses seeming slightly more interested in their bread than their circuses, President Great repeats the lie that more than 3 million people voted "illegally," costing him the popular vote, a result that does not conform with his image of himself.

The next day, President Great's Press Secretary, The Troll, reiterates President Great's false assertion that more than 3 million people voted "illegally," costing President Great the popular vote.

The next day President Great mistakenly tweets a photo from a massive Women's Protest March on Washington, saying it will hang in the White House Press Room and represent the crowd he wished had attended his inauguration.

That same day, President Great orders the Environmental Protection Agency to stop communicating with the public through social media or the press, and to freeze all grants and contracts. Then President Great orders the United States Department of Agriculture to stop communicating with the public through social media or the press without White House vetting, and to stop publishing any papers or research. Then his Director of the Department of Health and Human Service nominee characterizes federal guidelines on transgender equality as "absurd."

Then President Great orders the resumption of construction on a violently unpopular Pipeline, and the legislature of the great state of North Dakota considers a bill that would legalize striking Pipeline protesters with cars if they're on roadways. (It's a public safety issue, etc.)

Then President Great announces he's going to build a wall between the United States and Mexico, and ban Muslims from entering America — and, in my next chapter, President Great announces he's going to build a wall between the United States and Canada and ban the National Hockey League from playing games in Edmonton.

OK. Maybe that last one is a bit too broad. But, otherwise, how you liking "Great!" so far?

How the Revolution Started (Bank Guard)

He's outfitted for combat:

Ankle boots; black dungarees; Sam Browne belt with cuffs and mace and other tools of the craft; bulletproof vest; sunglasses; implacable stare.

And a gun, holstered at the moment.

The nametag says whatever you want it to say.

He's standing in the parking lot, guarding the bank, where inside there must be more money than the security officer will earn in his lifetime.

Sometimes he imagines with a sense of wonderment the origin of all that he protects: Where did it come from? And then this is the part he always returns to, like a reliable reading spot: What did all those people streaming through the doors that he oversees and protects --how did they get it?

What did they do? What was their trick?

Besides being born here?

He is paid very much more than what he would be paid in the place where he came from.

In Los Angeles, he's paid somewhat more than the governmentally decreed mandatory minimum. Which is only right.

Guarding other people's money is dangerous work.

Putting your life on the line every day for a Bank, a biggie, an important one that, from what he hears, was somehow responsible for the recession – well, that could get you killed.

So $15.75 per hour (or whatever amount you wish to represent a fair and decent wage), on most days seems about right. But today a thought occurred to the Bank Guard:

What would happen?

When he's on duty he's responsible. No deputies. No backup. When he has to go, to pee, like any person must eventually -- what would happen?

Usually he positions himself behind the hatchback of his car, parked butt side against a low wall demarcating the Bank's property, over which he is the lone Armed Protector. He wedges himself between the car and wall and opens the trunk and retrieves a worn paper cup, *grande* size a Bank customer once mentioned, and looking, scanning his dominion, still doing his job, the one that pays him the amount that you think is correct given the known circumstances, he relieves himself into the cup, his hands and gun belt demurely obscured, swivelhead and badge still visible. Still protecting all the money.

When bladder's empty, he dumps the warm piss,
Mountain Dew color this day, over the wall, onto the
grass.

Then he returns the cup to its waiting place. He
cannot return to work because he never left, and
there's pride to be taken or found in that somewhere
we can all agree.

But what would happen, the Bank Guard muses, his
penis between thumb and fingers, aimed down like an
udder, what would happen if something happened?

What would happen if trouble arrived while he was in
mid-stream?

An incident. Protesters. Robbers. Intruders upon the
turf he is paid to defend.

What would happen if he failed to shoot them with his
gun?

What if he watched serenely, the foam rising and his
cup hand warming, awake and seeing clearly now,
with thoughts of violence swarming, and, instead of
harming, he surveyed the property, zipped himself
properly, withstood the dark comedy, behaved
unheroically, maybe undemocratically and certainly
disreputably —

What if he walked long and slow and unhurriedly back
home to his wife's pillowy embrace to make love with
her all afternoon and into the evening?

We can't all *be rich, you know!*
Without a permanent lower caste,
who will serve?

-The Termite Squad

How Money Works

Let's simplify things. There are whole books, 100-pagers, devoted to the subject of our monetary system. About how it actually works. Lots of details. I'll just boil it down to the main points.

Main one: Money, as you're probably aware, does not exist. Like many other "things" in our modern world, money is a "virtual" commodity. We all agree to assign this virtual commodity a value, but that value is utterly arbitrary and tied to nothing.

Since all the world's major banks, including China Bank™ and Bank of North America™, loan exponentially more money than they have on deposit, it's theoretically impossible to repay the world's outstanding debt to the banks. There isn't enough money in the overall supply to cover the principal and interest.

Where does the additional money supply come from? Our imagination. How does the money supply constantly grow? Because we print more money.

The banks print money, worth nothing, backed by nothing, except we collectively agree to say that it's worth something. They loan imaginary money and have real money (including foreclosed property and interest) repaid to them. When debtors can't pay – as we've seen recently with Greece and a many African debtor nations – the banks seize all the hard assets, the buildings and the infrastructure, and turn the "grateful" citizens into indentured servants.

Look at the tallest buildings in your city. Look at the names on the side of the buildings: Banks, insurance companies, accounting firms. The big money is in money. You trade a fictional commodity and end up owning very real property, known as real estate. You own everything and everyone.

Some call it organized crime. Some call it the American Way.

Corruption

Our dwindling reserve of human kindness and compassion, diluted and poisoned by nearly constant assault from the corroding force of cruelty, still becomes inflamed by the fuel of outrage when we receive reports of foul play, endemic unfairness, and rank injustice motivated by the eternal and constant tug of noxious human greed.

We blanch at oil companies happily accepting — and strenuously lobbying for — $4 billion in taxpayer subsidies.

We mutter disconsolate platitudes when we learn of Police Chiefs, City Administrators, and Heads of This and That behaving like common thieves.

We *tsk-tsk* at psychopathic dictators treating their oppressed subjects like so many indentured servants.

We fret over athletes injecting themselves with chemicals that help them be more perfect gladiators in our televised circuses

We get upset at those who refuse to play fair.

Yet every day most of us wake up wondering not how we can be of genuine service to someone other than ourselves but how we can get ahead of everyone else scrambling for the last seat on the lifeboat.

What's lost in our outrage and disappointment is that the hooligans and bullies who control the world's power, money, and property are playing by another set of rules, an unspoken but widely understood code of ethics. Our society, our species, is organized in a way that encourages and rewards those who exploit others. At that particular game the bribe-able government officials, lying corporate executives, and violent henchmen who prop them up on their esteemed pedestals are particularly accomplished. They've figured out how one wins while still keeping up appearances of propriety.

So long as we deify those who hoard (billionaires, multi-national corporations, most "royal" families) at the expense of virtually everyone else, masking the rotten stench of greed and megalomania with encomiums in praise of "family values" and "civic virtue," we tacitly encourage a system that is inherently corrupt.

Not only have we gotten from "free-market" capitalism what we deserve, we've gotten what we secretly want. Perish the day when all people, no matter where they were born or from whose loins they emerged, get a "proper education," or affordable health care, or nutritious food. For when that day comes, our fantasy of being rich, of having those below us on the hierarchy do all the actual work, will have been vanquished by the unpleasant downside to equality: there's no one left to exploit, except the planet's other species and the planet itself. (We're pretty good at that, too.)

If the idea is to profit from the labor of others, to maximize whatever advantages one enjoys over the next guy, what we commonly call "corruption" is just an un-sanitized form of business-as-usual.

We take great offense at blatant malefactors because they had the audacity to bypass all the formalities we Good and Decent folk rely on to excuse our own willingness to use our fellow humans for personal gain. Shame on them!

Shame on us, too. We participate in a system that's corrupt at its toxic core. We're the henchmen who allow the pigs to wallow. When they shit upon our shiny shoes, we ought not be surprised or outraged. We should be ready.

You know what they want? They want obedient workers, people who are just smart enough to run the machines and do the paperwork. People who are intellectually docile enough to accept their horrible job, to accept increasingly lower pay, longer hours, reduced benefits, and a vanishing pension.

- The Termite Squad

More Work + Less Money = Progress

A few fleeting years ago the United States economy recovered all of the jobs lost during the great Wall Street Recession.

But here's the even better news: The newly created jobs paid an average of 23% less than the ones lost in the "downsizing." According to a report issued by the United States Conference of Mayors based on 2012 Census data, higher-paying jobs in the construction and manufacturing sectors were replaced by jobs in the lower-paying sectors of healthcare and hospitality.

It gets better. From 2005 to 2012, the analysis shows, the top 20% of earners were responsible for more than 60% of all income gains in our fine and fair republic. The bottom 40% enjoyed a 6.5% increase.

You can call it "income inequality," or whatever other whiny euphemism you prefer. We call it "economic justice." You see, the members of our society who are the most important – the people who don't actually do physical labor – deserve to be rewarded with the most money. That's how our system works, of course. The most valuable among us get more of everything. The less valuable get less. What's so hard to understand about that? Instead of complaining, those of us far from the top ought to thank our betters for creating so many jobs.

You can invoke "all men are created equal" and other outmoded philosophies, but we all tacitly understand that life is a [insert your preferred metaphor here] war/game/race, and not everyone can win. Some of us are losers, and maybe we'd all be better off if everyone just accepted it.

We don't mean to suggest that a wider disparity in income between winners and losers is necessarily a good idea. If things get too out-of-whack – and when the peasantry realizes they'll never have a fraction of what their superiors own – the mob could be lulled out of its waking slumber to some sort of horribly unpleasant action, like voting. Or striking. Better to keep things the way they are, more or less. Let the chasm widen slowly, almost imperceptibly. It's harder to notice the ever-increasing distance that way, and by the time the uneducated and untalented and lazy come to their senses there will be a new TV show to binge-watch, and everyone will feel better.

The banks are bigger than ever. CEOs earn more than ever. Corporate profits are at historic highs, as are many stock market indices. The system is working. And so is America (for 23% less income than before, but let's not quibble). More folks than ever are learning to say, "Hi, my name is [name] and I'll be your server today," and, really, isn't helping others what our capitalist system is all about?

Zombies Are Blameless, and So Are We

If you voluntarily buy burritos from Chipotle or pay for TV programs owned by Discovery, companies whose CEOs earn 1,000 times more than the average employee they oversee, then you probably don't have any problem with wealth and income inequality. You're certainly not going to have a problem with all the other corporations, like, for instance, Disney, where the Executives-to-Workers ratio is in the hundreds. Indeed, you recognize that corporations do so much good for the world in their relentless pursuit of profit and growth that you're willing to overlook the naked greed of the (mostly) white men siphoning off millions in profits for themselves and their precious families while everyone else does the actual work. On you shop, not exactly oblivious but more-or-less unbothered.

If you love America, then you believe in capitalism. If you love capitalism, there's never been a better time to be alive. You're presently in a state of something akin to modern nirvana. The machine is working perfectly. The worthiest, most valuable members of our society are being rewarded lavishly for the greatness they refract among the rest of us. Money is flowing upward – and has been for decades – the way it's supposed to in a system that operates outside of the Laws of Nature.

Money wins. Capital triumphs. Industry vanquishes sloth.

For many of us, the truth about how we've allowed ourselves to be organized is too painful. We can't look at our beloved husband or daughter or grandson and see a pig at the trough. We can't look ourselves in the mirror and cop to the fact that we participate every day in a society that systematically (and predictably) relegates many of our brothers and sisters to a life of indentured servitude and second-class citizenry. So we watch zombie shows. We tweet about zombie shows. We "like" someone's comment about themselves watching a zombie show, appended to an IG selfie, "Can't tell who the real zombies r anymore!" #couchspud

We fill the holes in our soul with triple-stuffed-nacho-burger-wings (and "organic" burritos that are making fellows in an office very rich). We scream at the television when the sub-literate genetic freak drops the ball and "our" team fails to be the best. We vacation somewhere fabulous, where the locals are exotic and grateful for American consumption. We "relax." We take care of ourselves, because lord knows the American healthcare gulag won't.

On some level we *kinda sorta* understand that all the money we spend on weapons of mass mayhem could be spent on other things, like education and healthcare. But on another level we feel a vague sense of relief that there's a productive use for all the bad students not smart enough to sit at a desk and issue directives.

Are things perfect? Not quite. But we must acknowledge that no one is breaking any laws. (OK, at least no one is going to jail for it). Everyone is playing by the rules. And the rules say that our society is built like a pyramid. We all need to find two or more people below us so we (and our dear children) can have more than the losers who stir the beans at Chipotle.

Maybe illegal immigration isn't such a bad deal after all...

We as a society don't really truly want to educate everyone excellently. The elites require servants and people to clean up after them.

- The Termite Squad

How the Revolution Started (Nanny)

How obvious is the adoration she has for this child,
the one she chaperones around the neighborhood in a
$1,400 stroller?

Her smile radiates a shroud of love over the low
chariot, protecting the sleeping boy inside, oblivious
to what we sometimes call reality. Oblivious as his
parents, who pay her to push their son. The parents
who crow to their friends, "We pay her next to nothing
and she's grateful for it!"

She loves him as if he were her own. But on her worst
days, when the bus is late or crowded with handsy
men and garlic smells, when the dream she crafted
and believed and returned to faithfully, like a psalm,
becomes hard to see, fading, the screen cracking,
distorting, the story ending faster than she wanted –
on those dark angry no hope days when she feels like a
thundercloud, she wonders the worst.

She wonders: What kind of world is this where one
Lady goes to a job in which she sits in a chair and talks
on the phone, while the other lady, the one paid by the
phone talker, watches over the more important Lady's

child – while no one strolls with *her* child, *her* boy, the one she leaves at home in front of the TV games with her 82-year-old great aunt?

She knows, she feels in the deepest part of her chest, that her boy is worth just as much as the boy she watches for next-to-nothing gratefulness wages. That's when the rages boil, scalding the back of her vision. She's in no mood for decision making or new path taking. But when the wrongness brings her nearer to tears than God, she allows herself a moment of precognition: She sees herself letting go. Washing her hands of the whole business. Relieved.

The sleeping boy will be OK, she's sure, for, yes, it's true what you saw: she loves him as if he were her son.

But on the day the revolution started, in her new vision. She lets go and now he's rolling down the hill on all four wheels, all green lights, straight shot down the slope to the office building where his mother will be waiting to catch him, ready to realize she has a son. And so does *she*. And so do all the "shes."

And each child is the most important baby in the world.

Thank You, Bernie Sanders

Thank you, Bernie Sanders, for your leadership.

Thank you, Bernie Sanders, for your courage, your authenticity, your compassion.

Thank you, Bernie Sanders, for speaking truth to power. Thank you for rousing the sleeping giant. Thank you for proving conclusively that progressive ideas aren't frivolous and "out there" but mainstream and sensible.

America is awakening. America is seeing through the greed and cynicism it's been falsely assured is inevitable, a "necessary" part of modern life. Citizens who had previously been thoroughly disenchanted with politics are listening carefully and watching closely. And life in the United States will never be quite the same.

Just as the Occupy Wall Street movement of 2008 changed the national conversation, this election cycle has transformed the national political consciousness.

Because of the Bernie Sanders campaign, we collectively understand how profoundly corrupted our political system is. Now we understand how undemocratic the two dominant political parties are.

How the Revolution Started:
Essays and Impertinent Thoughts

Now we understand (too well) that the "news media" are merely entertainment portals in search of ratings and advertisers, and that everything we've been told by those alleged "trusted experts" is about as credible as a children's fairy tale.

Now we know: America is controlled by a small cabal of oligarchs and their compliant bag-carriers. But now we also know that the people — everyone who will never sit on the Board of Wal-Mart, or collect bribes in the form of "speaking fees," or own a private prison – *the people* are the biggest corporation of all. And we can't be stopped.

I'm one of those people. I'm 51; I have no children; I'm financially well-off compared to the average American; I collect no government benefits and very few services; I personally do not need a $15-an-hour minimum wage, or Medicare-for-all, or paid maternity leave, or tuition-free education. I stand to gain nothing from a Bernie Sanders presidency – except the knowledge that my country, for the first time in my life, is finally headed on a path toward peace, kindness, and inclusiveness.

Like many of my fellow Americans, I've had enough war. I've had enough racism and sexism and jingoism. And like many of my fellow Americans, I'm no longer willing to let neoliberal corporate apologists pass themselves off as progressive agents of change.

Until Bernie Sanders declared his intention of running for President without corporate or PAC support, I hadn't donated to or volunteered for a political campaign; they were all versions of the same product packaged differently. Bernie changed me. It has been one of the great pleasures of my life to donate and volunteer for his campaign —*our* campaign — to add another voice to a growing chorus of righteousness. Before I joined this spectacular grassroots effort and talked with voters on their doorsteps and the massive hordes at public rallies, I considered it unthinkable that someone running against the monolithic establishment machine could win the California primary funded by $27 donations.

The Lie has been exposed. From the moment Bernie Sanders announced his candidacy, business-as-usual cynics started spinning their plausible-sounding but mendacious story: *He can't win. I like him but he can't win. CNN told me he can't win.*

All the polls and the math and people in suits who sound like they know what they're talking about say he can't win. *He can't win.*

He can win. He *will* win. We the People will win.

The Clinton campaign and the corporations that supported her spent $200 million to convince gullible voters she's the "only" choice. What did all that money buy? A gradual and inexorable loss of her "insurmountable" lead and plunging approval ratings the more she appeared in public and was forced to answer difficult "yes or no" questions. Only the disastrous "War on Drugs" has returned less on its monetary investment.

How the Revolution Started:
Essays and Impertinent Thoughts

Whether or not the money launderers who run the Democratic Party have the good sense to one day nominate Bernie Sanders for President of the United States, this movement, this blossoming, will continue to flourish. It's too late to turn back or pretend that the-way-we've-always-done-it is acceptable.

Moral clarity has triumphed. Bernie Sanders – and the ideals he represents – has already won the hearts and minds of millions of voters who had given up on the process. And we're not going away.

Thank you, Bernie Sanders, for fundamentally changing our country. You are not alone. We're all in this together.

Immigration, Income, and Making America Great (Again)

Contrary to what Donald J. Trump and his followers claim to believe, immigration is not what's keeping America from being great (again). If folks who live in Iowa and New Hampshire who are convinced that our national safety rests on the construction of a giant wall between Mexico and what used to be Mexico – if they lived instead in, say, California, they would see that immigration isn't a pernicious cancer gnawing at the organs of our economy. They would see that immigration (legal or otherwise) is pretty great, because it keeps industries like agriculture, construction and restaurants running smoothly and with handsome profits for the (mostly white) non-immigrants who employ the (mostly brown) "guest workers."

America is a land of immigrants. Back around 1900, scapegoats were made of Italians and Irish and Poles. Now their great-grandchildren are finding convenient targets in Spanish speakers.

Back around 1850, immigration was difficult for the Cherokee and the Sioux, the Navajo and the Cree. Too bad for them that Donald J. Trump's ancestors, and a horde of other Europeans, were immigrating to (and on and over and all around) their native lands, later to be transformed into shopping malls and office towers.

Back around 1750, immigration was difficult for former residents of various African nations.

But they persevered. *We* persevered. All us immigrants figured out how to live among each other. And how to keep the mill wheel turning. The history of America teaches us that slaves, or indentured servants, must be procured from somewhere. *Someone* must do the labor and do it cheaply, otherwise how can the plantation owner enjoy a life of leisure and moral uplift? Our current strategy is a hybrid of outsourcing — to places like Bangladesh and Sri Lanka, or wherever else the locals will be grateful for a soul-crushing, repetitive, potentially dangerous job that pays a princely $3 a day — and in-sourcing, importing the cheap laborers from El Salvador and Guatemala and wherever else our imperialist meddling has destabilized lawful society and enriched violent oligarchs.

Our society's fascination with immigrants-as-malefactors dovetails nicely with the long-nascent, currently blossoming awareness of income inequality. They both seem to be the Essential Problem. But only one them really is.

If you're reading this, you probably consider you and your offspring way too smart to have to take a minimum-wage job. Those jobs are for teenagers and Mexicans (who stole all the good jobs away from industrious Americans). But you're also probably good enough at math to figure out how much someone earns who works 40 hours a week for $10-an-hour. You can probably also figure out what that person would earn if the minimum wage was raised to $15. Yes, $120 a day, $600 a week.

Raising a working person's income to around $30,000 from $20,000 will mean a demonstrable change in quality of life. But folks are worried about where the money will come from. Higher prices at Burger King? Less income for me? Here's all you need to know: Blue Shield, the allegedly non-profit insurer whose coffers have grown by billions of dollars thanks to the ACA boondoggle, awarded their top executives $64 million in compensation – you know, for managing things so excellently. No one broke any laws, so we can take comfort in the good character of the board members involved. We can also remind ourselves that this sort of chicanery occurs every day at every major corporation in America. And we the people pay for it.

So what if we collectively decided that what we prefer to pay for is a living wage for the people who do the jobs no one wants? What if we collectively decided we prefer for poor people at the bottom of the pyramid to have a drastically larger portion of the pie while people at the very top have slightly less?

Here's what would happen: America would be such a better place that immigration would increase rapidly and with such fervor that we would need a 12-foot wall encasing our borders.

Maybe Trump and his acolytes are right, after al

In the case of wealth – expressed as money and real estate and tangible assets – wealth is never distributed properly. It's not that we as a society, a civilization, a species, don't have enough wealth to go around so that every single living creature, every human and every animal, can have a dignified and peaceful existence here on this magnificent green planet. We have plenty. But the majority of that planetary wealth is held in the covetous hands of a genetically damaged few.

- The Termite Squad

The State Trooper Explains Standing Rock to His Child

"Daddy!"

"Welcome home from school, honey. How was your day, little girl? Did you learn a lot in Fourth Grade?"

"Yes, Daddy. I did."

"Like?"

"Our teacher talked about the savages who were living here way back when before normal Americans discovered America. The Indians. They rode horses and walked everywhere. They had different tribes. One of them is like a girl's name. The Susans. Pretty funny."

"Yes. The Sioux. Tribe of Sitting Bull."

"They had cute names like that. Crazy Horse! And they ate buffaloes."

"Buffalo meat ain't half bad, you know. You had it once. Remember? At the Hansen's barbecue? It's just

like beef when you grill it right. . . So, yeah, good.
Good day at school for my little princess."

"Yep. We learned there are a lot of Indians in our
state. How was your day, Daddy?"

"Oh, you know, Daddy is protecting people and
keeping sweet little girls like you safe from bad guys."

"Like bank robbers!"

"Yeah. Like that."

"You got a bank robber today? Oh, my God! I have to
tell Ashley."

"No, we didn't have no robberies today, sweetheart.
Nothing like that. I was out in the field, far away from
the bank."

"In a field?"

"Yeah, like a meadow. Out in the countryside, near the
river. Very pretty, actually. No bank robbers there as
far as I could tell."

"But you were still protecting people and keeping
them safe, right Daddy?"

"Oh, yes. Yes. Protecting and serving. Keeping it safe
for *everyone*, including you, honey girl. There are
people that do something called *vandalism*. You know
what that is? When you write on a wall? Or spray
paint something? So, where your daddy's working

lately, there are a lot of people like that. Vandals. My job is to stop them."

"The water protec—"

"*Vandals.* The vandals who want to destroy public property that's allowed to be where it is. I make sure everyone follows the rules. Now, see, I don't make the rules. I just make sure the rules are respected. And if they don't respect the law. . ."

"You shoot them!"

"No, no, no, silly. Daddy doesn't have to use his gun except for bank robbers. I stop them other ways."

"All my friends know my dad is so brave! Thank you, Daddy, for being a hero."

"You're welcome, princess."

"Thank you for protecting us."

"That's what I do."

That's pretty much the way things work. If they want you to know about it, you will. If they don't, you won't. They're very good at controlling their messaging.

- The Termite Squad

How the Revolution Started (Street Poet)

No one is paying attention. But she doesn't care. She's a poet: being ignored is part of the job description. Thousands of people, mostly tourists, stream past her Speaker's Corner in the heart of Hollywood. One day, she imagines, they will awaken. And then what?

Until then, she tells herself: *speak the truth and everything else will take care of itself.*

Ready to do her work, eager to share, the Street Poet steps up and on her box –a soapbox, for real. She clears her throat and begins to recite from memory.

WHEN IS WHEN

When the Commander-in-Chief volunteers his firstborn child
to be an armed first-responder as the next school shooting erupts,
to lead the infantry charge in Afghanistan,
to affirm with the sacrifice of their privileged life the righteousness of the cause
that is when I will support military intervention.

When every child, regardless of anything, is the most important baby in the world
because every human life is miraculous,
because where you were born does not matter,

because your hordes of cash or melatonin or religious superstitions are
irrelevant
that is when the world will begin to live as one.

When the profit motive is removed from healthcare
   and education
   and criminal justice
   and everything else
that is when we begin,
hoping to do a wee bit better on the do-over.

IGNORANCE IS BLISS

We manage to live here
   mostly voluntarily
in a country whose concept of
Justice
is: Murder the miscreants
   with injections or gas or gallows.
Call it "execution." Call it "capital punishment."
The "death penalty," not the Death Penalty.
We mean it euphemistically, you see.
Kill the convicts who deserve to die
   we dutifully declare.
But however and yet we've carved out
   a beautiful caveat
      for those we call retarded or mentally disabled
         those who can
         take a test
            an IQ test
         and prove
         to us, their juries and future killers, that
         although they are criminals
            they are not
            intelligent enough to die.

CAPITALISM EXPLAINED, KIND OF

The less I participate
The better I feel
Unrighteous organizational scheme dictating and demanding
    An imperative like parched lungs drinking air
    A guarantee a requirement a certainty
That there shall be constant waste
That immeasurable resources and countless lives be squandered
In order for everything to work perfectly

Surely you've been told by a person of authority
There's nothing wrong in making a profit
When you were younger that sounded right
Even if it didn't really

You hadn't yet compiled a lifetime of evidence
    An amicus brief on behalf of the People
    The People vs a system most wouldn't choose
    if they had a choice

This poem is not for sale
It will be given away freely and unbound
No one will have been exploited in its creation
Not for a hummingbird moment
Especially not the author

Finished with her performance, the Street Poet accepts a smattering of applause and steps down from her box. She gathers and counts the donations left in a cardboard container marked "Donate Here."

The people have left her $1.44 this morning. She's encouraged.

When you think about it, that's the way things are supposed to work. The most valuable people got the money, not the interchangeable ones on the bottom, the ones who we don't value and who don't deserve it.

- The Termite Squad

Resistance Action Plan

How are you resisting?

We've been asked this question often. How are you resisting "the occupation?" The "fascist state?"

Knowing fully how woogie-woogie the answer sounds, we sometimes make a joke about having nothing to resist, what with the current administration's glaring and obvious kindheartedness, how everything they do is informed by care and compassion.

The truth is, we're "resisting" the same way we resisted the last three administrations: by meeting ugliness and hatred with beauty and love.

Barf! (Please note: A woogie-woogie warning was properly posted.)

When faced with divisiveness, we seek unity. When faced with un-Christian behavior, we remember the teachings of Christ. Everything we see lacking in our leaders — a modicum of human decency, to name one — we try to replace threefold what's lacking in ourselves. Their flaws are our flaws; the difference is we choose to fix ours.

How the Revolution Started:
Essays and Impertinent Thoughts

So, for every revolutionary out there, everyone who refuses to abdicate to rage and resentment, we unveil our brief and exceedingly simple 2017 Resistance Action Plan. This is the scheme were currently using. Feel free to change the world by changing yourself, or don't. This unchecked aggression will not stand.

We resist.

RESISTANCE ACTION PLAN

+ Stop looking for kindness and virtue in your fellow human beings. Start being kind and virtuous to your fellow human beings.

+ Find the least among you and care for them as though they were your own child (or pet).

+ Speak truth to power and be compassionate when you do, because power is frightened of truth.

+ Understand that there's enough of everything for everyone; generosity will not cause anyone to suffer.

+ Be the version of You you wish to become.

+ Make a giant pot of soup and share

Looking Back on 2012: An Oral History of American Values

I was young like you once. Don't laugh. It seems impossible, I know. An old codger like me of 77! You probably can't picture when I was only 47 and healthy, with all my own teeth and a libido that didn't yet require boner pills.

Sure, that was three decades ago, and I look a lot different, what with the thinning hair, sloping shoulders, and cute little pot belly. But my memory is still sharp, even with all that weed I smoked. I remember perfectly what we were like 30 years ago, back in '12, and I'm glad your professor asked you to do this project. I'm glad you're talking to the older generation. Folks like me know what America was like back then, back in the time of Obama. The USA was different.

How do I mean? Well, even in 2012, which isn't really that long ago in the grand scheme, America was still a mean-spirited country. This century! *Progressive* was a dirty word. There were still a surprising – and frightening – number of people whose beliefs you younger ones would find archaic. Or despicable, depending on how polite you want to be with your old uncle.

Back in 2012, a large part of the population – mostly people who identified themselves as Christians – believed that homosexuals shouldn't have the same rights as heterosexuals. There were even big companies that got involved, trying to get legislation passed to outlaw marriages. Adult marriages, I mean. Those companies are all out of business now, of course. But back then if you hated gay people you expressed your prejudices by spending your money at gay-hating businesses. That year some chicken restaurant stumbled into politics. They felt that they had to take a position and stand up for God, because, you know, His omniscience isn't what it used to be. Sorry, I can't recall their name today. But I'm sure you can look it up on the eyepiece thing you're always wearing.

Yeah, the iris screen. That thing.

And speaking of chickens, here's another fact: Back in 2012 – you're not going to believe this – people still accepted food that was factory produced.

Oh, yes. I'm not kidding! With the antibiotics and the feces and the cruelty. And vegetables – oh, this is funny. Do you know that they used to label food "organic"?

Yes, they did!

No, they didn't label the stuff with cancer-causing chemicals on it "inorganic." They just put labels on properly cultivated food and charged twice as much for it.

You actually paid, like, twice as much for the kind of food we all eat today. Back in '12, you could still get cancer-causing foods cheap, without any of the excise taxes – we used to call them "sin taxes" when it was cigarettes and alcohol. And believe me, we were *fat.* I mean fat! Like morbidly obese. No, not a few freaks. I mean most Americans. I'm sure you've seen the pictures. Sad. But also sort of funny, too, right? The self-poisoning thing?

[*inhales deeply from a water pipe; offers to interviewer*] And...as you well know...since it's only been...How many years?...[*exhales*] Right. Less than ten. Yeah. Less than ten years ago cannabis was still illegal in some States.

Back in '12? [*laughs*] Ha! Thirty years ago the Feds were still busting medical patients.
Yes! Obama! Barack Hussein Obama. His Justice Department.

I'm certain about the dates. I wrote a book about marijuana around that time, when he was in his first term. It was strange: In 2012, even some of the smartest people in America still believed all the 20th Century lies about weed. The propaganda.

Even Mr. Obama. That, obviously, was before Malia came down with multiple sclerosis...

[*sighs*] Fate can be cruel. But so can we humans. Do you know that back when I was younger, up until my 60s, we put people in prisons at a higher rate than any other country in the world? When I say 'any other country' I'm including all the repressive, dictatorial regimes crushing their opponents in the courts. We were the grand champions of incarceration! That all changed when pot was legalized and the private prison industry went bankrupt. The Corrections Industry, I believe it was called.

[*laughs*] Isn't that funny? At one time, earlier this century, warehousing your fellow citizens behind bars was the fastest-growing business in America. But the convict factories were the victim of weak demand. Adam Gopnik wrote that book about it – what was it? *Cages & Capitalism?*...Yeah, a real mind-changer. Like the Upton Sinclair book, and the Rachel Carson book...I guess we're capable of getting hip. We just like to take our time about it.

Speaking of businesses, do you know that we used to allow corporations to pollute our water and air and not pay for it?

Yes. That was the attitude back then.

"Environmentalist" was a term of derision. People accepted poison in their air and water because they'd been conditioned to think about low prices instead of their children and grand-children.

How the Revolution Started:
Essays and Impertinent Thoughts

I suppose that continues to this day. You've still got
your climate change deniers and your radical free-
marketeers, your little cults of ignorance. But back in
'12, there were more of them than you might imagine.
[*chuckles*] My generation! Embarrassing.

The biggest difference between then and now?

Well, I was going to say the merger of the Republican
and Democratic parties into the New America Party
five years ago. But in my recollection, even thirty years
ago when they were still going through the motions of
opposing each other, everyone knew that they were
both suckling at the corporate teat. We used to call the
Republicans and Democrats the 'Money Party' before
they formally merged. So I suppose things aren't
much different now than back then.

The biggest change, I think, is that back in 2012, the
elderly didn't have any legal rights to manage their
death. No government-supplied suicide kit. No
familial blessing to go early than later. No dignity. It
was awful, as I'm sure you've heard.

I don't think there was a single catalyst, one explosive
event that swayed public opinion. But I remember
there being a lot of talk about termites.

Yes, termites.

The wood-eating insects. Those.

Well, I'm not sure if it was a book or a Pixar movie, but
Termite Method became a catch phrase. You were either

in favor of keeping the infirm elderly alive to live meaningless lives or you were for the *Termite Method*. Which was, basically, a trait that scientists discovered about termites in 2012. That's when the whole paradigm shifted.

What the scientists discovered was that certain termite species sent their elderly – male and female – on suicide missions. They literally blew themselves up through the abdomen. These toxic explosions blocked invaders from conquering the home nest.

This was a step beyond what used to be called the *Eskimo Way*, which involved the elderly voluntarily leaving the igloo and ending their life alone on an ice floe. The *Termite Method* went further. Not only could you get rid of unwanted old people – particularly Baby Boomers, the worst – you could make them feel supremely useful and selfless as they said farewell to life.

The Martyr Brigade that took down the Iranian nuclear facilities in 2029 was definitely from the *Termite Method* school of thought. And the American suicide bombers that killed that Chinese colony planner on the tour bus? They all would have been in nursing homes. Now they're heroes and we build statues of them.

Me? Oh, I've got the pill. [*chuckles*] When the time is right.

President Trump
and Beyond

Shock. Disbelief. Catatonia. We've observed various
forms of post-traumatic stress disorder manifested in
Hillary Clinton voters, very few of whom seem able to
process the idea that the fiasco we witnessed
unfolding in slow-motion was an election, not a
coronation.

We've heard the tearful confessions: "I'm speechless."
"I'm frightened." "I'm so upset I think I might rouse
myself from my usual cycle of acquire-consume-
repeat and actually, like, call someone to complain."

We saw in person a master comedian, T.J. Miller,
sputter through a laughless stand-up set in which he
attempted to "process" his hurt feelings. We read a
tortured editorial in *The New Yorker* in which smart
and educated writers attempted to explain how
Donald J. Trump confounded the polls and the pre-
election pronouncements offered by smart and
educated publications like *The New Yorker,* one of
dozens of media outlets (CNN, the *Washington
Post,* the A.P., MSNBC, the *New York Times*, the
national TV broadcast networks, *etc., etc.*) that has yet
to fully take responsibility for anointing Hillary
Clinton the next President — during the primaries,

when another candidate, Bernie Sanders, was making a devastating case against her war-for-profit worldview. Clinton's claque dismissed him, ridiculed him and actively schemed against him, helping to deliver the presidency to a reality TV clown.

We've seen a lot of finger-pointing and not much mirror-looking.

Indeed, the enormous number of Democrats who are outraged, disgusted and energized *now*, as opposed to when this election was being rigged in Clinton's favor by the DNC and their state machines, gives us hope. These folks were asleep. Now they've been awakened. These folks were told repeatedly that their candidate was at best a coin-flip against Trump while Sanders soundly beat him in every poll extant. Now they've been awakened. These folks were told that those of us who don't participate in, or profit from, the global oligarchy were compelled to support the foul state of affairs — because, you know, the alternative was... [insert favorite groupthink phrase here.] Now we must all live with the consequences of their arrogance.

We don't care much for Donald J. Trump, except as a Falstaffian jester slightly more entertaining than a costumed professional wrestler. We agree with him on several key points (global trade deals; interventionist foreign wars; Wall Street kleptomania); we disagree with him on almost everything else. Cheerleaders for Trump we are not. Indeed, we happily voted for Jill Stein, which felt great, because all our latent misogyny had been spent opposing Clinton. We're Berniecrats. Our hearts and minds are with Bernie Sanders. So it might come as a surprise to those who share our progressive values that we're actually excited for the Trump Presidency.

Just as the Obama Presidency reshaped our conception of what's possible in America — namely, that even a *half*-white man can be an effective corporate stooge and constant war-maker — the Trump Presidency might prove that you really don't have to be a professional politician or trained bureaucrat to be the boss. We might discover that it really isn't necessary to know anything about anything (other than gaming the tax system) and still be in charge.

Obviously, it really was time to repudiate the status quo agenda offered by the Clinton Foundation. Sadly, the "party of change" put forth the most reviled establishment candidate of our lifetime instead of the most inspiring candidate of our lifetime. If Clinton would have won, implementing the systemic changes our republic needs would have been forestalled at best and impossible at worst. With Trump in office, millions of engaged Bernie voters will be joined by millions of newly conscious Clinton voters, and Senator Sanders, or a revolutionary candidate like him, will become the clear and convincing alternative to whatever mayhem Trump and Company are able to wreak between now and 2020. When everything comes into focus.

For the next four years, each citizen will have a daily opportunity to define her values, to ask himself "what kind of person am I hoping to one day become?" to identify leaders who represent the better angels of our nature. The next time we the people get to choose a President (and the shape of our national narrative,) we surely will be less confused, less complacent and less willing to accept more of the same.

That's how you turn hindsight into foresight.

Mass Disturbances: Future Law or Fatal Flaw

The future will probably breed disaster for the majority of people not connected to the ruling minority. The calamity won't be from a global plague or asteroid impact, or even atomic war – although those are all reasonable things to worry about. (Well, not the asteroid.)

What's worrisome is the obvious evolution of law enforcement from constabulary force to military force. Our current administration, and surely ones to come, treats the legal system as a cudgel and the police as a baton. Eventually, the force applied against peaceful Water Protectors and non-violent student protesters and anyone else who threatens the status quo will be applied to citizens in general, the awakened plebian masses unpacified by bread and circuses.

It feels like yesterday, back in '14, when I was at my once-upon-a-time job as an editor, sitting with my coworker at the News Bureau, when suddenly: an explosion.

We both dashed to my office window. On the street below, regular citizens were scurrying everywhere.

Hundreds, maybe thousands, of National Heroes were filling Central Avenue. But on this morning they weren't marching. They were dashing, running, streaming out of personnel carriers, wearing protective gas masks, swarming like emerald bees. I could hear agitated shouting, but I couldn't make out what was being said. When I saw all traffic pulling to the side of the avenue, and bystanders of all classification assuming the Safety Position – squatting in place, arms hugging the legs, face down on the knees -- I understood that our Sacred Homeland was undergoing a Security Emergency.

I heard another distant explosion, and then the official recording coming from loudspeakers: "Warning: Assume the Safety Position! Warning: Assume the Safety Position!"

We all squatted, with our heads down, a field of compliant human mushrooms.

And now we are all safer than we've ever been. And isn't that a good enough reason for anything?

More People in Metal Cages = A Better America

The new rankings just came out. We win again!

Of all the nations on Earth, the United States of America incarcerates the largest percentage of its population. Out of every 100,000 people, we put 716 in some kind of jail. No other civilized country is even close.

Nor are the uncivilized ones. Almost 25% of the entire world's behind-bars population is housed in an American *corrections facility* – so named because we're correct to warehouse unwanted blacks, druggies, and other assorted losers in human zoos.

Let's be clear: We don't have the world's largest prison population because America is a nation of criminals. It's not that we have more bad people than they do in other places. It's just that we're better at apprehending, convicting, and sentencing our bad people than everywhere else.

This is something to be proud of. Just when it seemed no one could take America seriously anymore — what with our hypocritical doublespeak on Egypt, our inability to bully other countries into handing over our political enemies, and the general creeping suspicion that people in India, Brazil and other "developing nations" might soon have as much buying power (and all the cool stuff that come with it) as us — the prison results came in. The winner, by a mile, was a beautiful country known by the moniker "the land of the free." Hooray and huzzah.

Other nations try to pass themselves off as havens of civility, places where Law and Order is a way of life, not a television program. China, Russia, various Central American dictatorships – they all claim to respect the Rule of Law. But none of them have built entire industries out of storing away undesirable citizens. They bandy about the honorific "police state," but they haven't really earned it.

We have. Rwanda (527 per 100K) is nipping at our heels. But they simply don't possess our wealth. They may have plenty of naughty citizens in need of jailing, but Rwanda just can't build as many prisons as us. Plus, they're busy rebuilding their nation after a couple of genocides, so we forgive them if they don't show as much devotion to law enforcement as America.

The Cayman Islands, what's their excuse? At only 382 per 100K (good enough to sneak into the top-20), this little Caribbean nation might want to tighten up their notoriously loose banking laws. That is, if they want their governmental authority to be taken seriously.

Not long ago, bowing to pressure from the increasingly powerful Cannabis Lobby, Attorney

How the Revolution Started:
Essays and Impertinent Thoughts

General Eric Holder, addressing the American Bar Association, announced plans for drug-sentencing reform. Holder's blueprint includes plans to divert low-level drug offenders to treatment programs and to release elderly, non-violent offenders. Holder clearly has no interest in upholding American prestige in the incarceration community. Indeed, Holder, who previously could be counted on to raid state-approved medical marijuana dispensaries, sounded as though he might be playing for another team: "We need to ensure that incarceration is used to punish, deter and rehabilitate – not merely to convict, warehouse and forget," Holder said. "Although incarceration has a role to play in our justice system, widespread incarceration at the federal, state and local levels is both ineffective and unsustainable. It imposes a significant economic burden — totaling $80 billion in 2010 alone — and it comes with human and moral costs that are impossible to calculate."

Impossible to calculate? If we had a dollar for every sweet child sleeping safely in the security of their parents' home, able to dream sweet dreams and awake without the threat of violence from some violent marijuana user – well, then we would be very rich, indeed.

Some radical provocative types discern a nefarious link between a nation with the world's largest military budget, the world's largest prison population, and a dual justice system for rich and poor. We don't. What we see is a country that realizes the more people you put in metal cages, the better off everyone who isn't in a metal cage will be.

How the Revolution Started:
Essays and Impertinent Thoughts

If you're an American who cares about American Values, the question you've got to ask yourself is: Do you want to be a winner, or do you want to be a loser (loser being defined as anything that's not a winner, winner being defined as first place)? Do you want America to be a nation where drug users are free to walk the streets, as though they were upstanding bankers or politicians?

Or do you want America to be a place that knows where to throw its filth?

#WeAreOne. Really?

You've seen the hashtags: #NotMeUs; #WeAreOne; #StrongerTogether.

They're all useful shorthand for complex ideas. So is "unity." On a "normal" day of "normal" news, the concept of *unity* strikes most of us as a thoroughly uncontroversial acclamation of cooperation and fellowship. Great. Sure.

What happens, though, when someone drives a truck into dozens of families?

What happens when terrorists terrorize, when violators violate, when haters hate? What happens when someone behaves as though he's inhuman? All those hashtags feel impotent and vaguely ridiculous. #WeAreOne? Really?

Yes. We are. Really.

Just as the First Amendment is most devoutly honored when we permit and accept hideously vile forms of speech, the concept of global unity – of universal harmony – is most devoutly honored when we refuse to label despicable malefactors as *Them*, as the dreaded *Other*. The temptation is to think of murderers as substantially different from the average human being, that reprehensible killers are zombie mutants, a debased sub-species of human that's not really human at all.

But it's not true. We know that the men who commit mass shootings and suicide bombings are bad, that they've committed Evil. We would probably say that about someone who killed fewer people, too. We would probably say that about someone who killed one person. Some might even say that about someone who kills only herself. And although it's difficult to identify exactly where, at some point in our deductive reasoning we recognize that takers of human life can sometimes be rehabilitated and forgiven. We do it every day with our soldiers and police; we might even congratulate them for their bravery. Somehow we understand that being a killer doesn't make you inhuman at all. It makes you a deeply flawed human being (or a hero, depending on your ideology).

Imperfect. Just like us. Like me. And maybe you. In the world's darkest moments, when peace and unification seem impossible and naïve, that's when we must open our hearts widest, recognizing that at one time or another we've all had hateful, destructive thoughts. Maybe we've harbored violent fantasies of retribution and revenge. Some of us may have even lived out our fantasy during the televised "shock and awe" phase of the Iraq War. Or "Game of Thrones." Or "Call of Duty."

Most of us, though, choose kindness over cruelty. We understand that healthy people don't behave violently,

How the Revolution Started:
Essays and Impertinent Thoughts

even if they have violent thoughts. We know – we
don't have to be told on Twitter, we *know* – that the
only answer to hate is overwhelming love and
compassion. For *everyone,* not merely for those who
look like us or speak the same language or were born
in the same general place or under the same zodiac
sign.

Love *everyone.* This is the fundamental principle of
all the world's religions, of progressive politics, of
every social movement in search of peace and justice.
To take care of each other, to truly be our brother's
keeper, we must first be brothers. To care for the least
among us, to truly heed the words of Jesus and
Buddha, we must consciously, willfully choose love
and compassion, even when confronted with
seemingly obvious examples of the Other – mass
murderers, Bashir Assad, Donald Trump.

They're awful, reprehensible, disgusting – whatever
adjective describes your outlook. But they're not the
Other. They're us on our very worst days, only more
so. How much only you can say.

In the face of what currently feels like overwhelming
anger and malice, shining the bright light of love is
more crucial than ever. Be courageous. The world
needs you. *You* need you.

And, yes, we need each other. All of us: the horrible
and the hideous, the gorgeous and adorable, the
pathetic and the piteous. We're all in this unknowable
mystery together.

Progress versus greed is what it boils down to. Meaning: People who actively suppress change, who actively stymie the worldwide impulse toward social justice, are usually quite happy with the way things are. Who wants to change when you're rich? When you're ahead? When you've won?

-The Termite Squad

Five-Sided Story

This is merely a minor reminder mainly meant to catapult adults into jolts of obvious offense or obstreperous discontent. At least that's the expected result!

This is *not* a jabbing joking jibe. This is not a fleet-footed treatise about bad vibes.

My proudly patriotic friends gathered before us, this is not an insolent insult. Put plainly, for the most unenlightened dolt: There's no dictionary you could consult, no thesaurus or magic lexicon that defines the Pentagon as a paragon of peace.

More like the patron saint of paramilitary police.

More like a massive factory churning out passive-aggressive offensives that inevitably end in disastrous catastrophes at distant Middle Eastern addresses.

More like Hollywood and Silicon Valley's most important ally in comprehensively convincing the populous that what's best for us is constant war and murderous mayhem on foreign shores.

How the Revolution Started:
Essays and Impertinent Thoughts

Excuse my jargon, but they try to make a trillion dollars seem like a bargain. Here's a harbinger of what's to come: We will not kneel and we will feel lethal and there will be no cost too high, because all would be lost without the KY tube of lubricating grease on the gangrene gears of our economy, stuck and stymied without an enemy to offend or a homeland to defend from [fill in the blank], pajama-clad *jihadis*, seductive Chinese hotties, or imperialistic Russian oligarchs owning all the best Bugattis – or Bentleys, or whatever wondrous wheels are suitable for those whose feudal evil is horribly immutable and deplorably inscrutable, yet reliably refutable by heavyweight wrestling champions of the world who specialize in sealing deals by euthanizing enthusiastic heels.

It wasn't always war-around-the-clock.

Before Afghanistan and Iraq, in the halcyon days before Iran and Vietnam, a quiet calm fell between the bombs.

Back then, we buffoons assumed the United States was safe, immune from the impending arms race. After receiving the vaccine, we ought not to have got autism or measles, or a feeble eating disorder in which the citizenry is feeding on fear, a diet of insecurity and pure hostility toward those who don't fully grok the power of a grenade or Glock versus our stock F-16, locked and loaded with a payload designed for *mujahidin*.

You know who I mean: uncivilized civilians with frivolous pavilions built from oil millions, scary Arabs who don't comprehensively comprehend America's transparently inherent right to bully anyone with insufficient humility or ironic mirth.

You know: the towel-heads and Commies who refuse to bow or *kow-tow* when confronted by the greatest country on earth.

Here's a useful fact if you want to keep track of the attack on truth maliciously instigated before you were born but 'til this day still quite the norm. Up until 1949 – World War II ended just before -- what we now call the Department of Defense answered to its proper name: The Department of War.

Hence, the Orwellian locution. War becomes defense.

The most reliable solution to a public relations debacle is to block all calls for truth-seeking, heat-leaking leaders. Just neatly repeat the Big Lie *ad infinitum*.

Here's one: You can't negotiate with "terrorists," you can only fight 'em.

Most of us intuitively understand in our glands, down to our pituitary, that we can't really "defend' America by making war on faraway "enemies" behind every muddy door.

We know we have a predilection for aggression and an addiction to violence (and pain pills and porn and muscle relaxers). Yet what we do with our knowledge doesn't compute: Stay mute and polite and keep nodding your head.

Nobody likes to be called "unpatriotic," a detractor from the grand larceny that we call American Democracy. But if you need a reason to declare my reasoning treasonous, I'll save you the time: Every nuclear device is a war crime waiting to happen, and every soldier in our military is a poorly paid mercenary exploited by the corporate salesmen whose quarterly profits will cost him his life. Or sight. Or, if he's lucky, PTSD, because, sure, it's a drag, but at least he can see and he didn't come home in a body bag, with a toe tag, wrapped up in an American flag.

If you want to mend a wound, sometimes you can't "stay tuned." You've got to filter out the noxious noise of popular culture and dial in the simple joys of poplars and maples and firs, the piquantly pleasurable treasures of mulch (or compost), of toasting the host of the universe, flirting with the chirping birds while moist dirt spurts from a formerly inert pile of detritus and flotsam that got some sun and some love and now nurtures the future with nutrients derived from decimated peanuts and desiccated daffodils, resuscitating human ills. On this fecund fertile growing ground, there's no Army or Marines, no drones or Humvees, no battle-ready death machines.

They say there's two sides to every story.

How the Revolution Started:
Essays and Impertinent Thoughts

When we talk about killing other humans so our
precious, precocious, intermittently atrocious
Republic can thrive, the story sides are always five.

But we can't give up. No abdication.

Let's add another wing to the dreary Pentagon. We'll
make it the Hexagon.

And we'll all sing a fairy hymn when We the People
create a new *Department of Peace* for our forlorn,
weary, war-torn nation.

Information – intelligence – is the currency. You learn quickly to hoard it (like everything else in this world) or else you lose it to someone else, and when you lose it you have nothing. You're not useful anymore. So people keep quiet.

\- The Termite Squad

Goodbye, Obama.
Hello, Trump.

The fearsome power to hurt many people for no good reason (and many bad ones) has passed from one very dangerous man to another very dangerous man.

At first blush, Donald Trump's brand of militarism appears more obnoxious, dunderheaded and foolish than his predecessor's brand of militarism. Specifically, the calls for updating the nuclear arsenal: Our species (and the species we speak for unilaterally) requires brave leaders everywhere to call for the abolishment of atomic weapons, not proliferation. Also troubling is the depressingly predictable nomination of Mr. Mad Dog to lead our "defense."

But make no mistake, Barack Obama proved to be as aggressively belligerent to the rest of the world as *his* predecessor, that great "War President" George W. Bush.

The Council on Foreign Relations reported that, in the last year of his Presidency, the peace-loving United States of America dropped 26,172 bombs on seven nations, most of them falling on what's left of Iraq and Syria, as well as the remainders of Libya. That comes out to about 3 bombs every hour, round-the-clock, keeping us safe and preserving our constantly threatened, cherished way of life. Paid for by your taxes. The ones that are too high to pay for national healthcare.

These bombs receive tacit endorsement from our collective unwillingness to take a different path. And so they continue to fall in my name. And yours.

Then again, all those bombs were ultimately being approved by a winner of the Nobel Peace Prize, and that part was altogether marvelous.

Perhaps the moment that Obama accepted his award in Oslo was when America officially began satirizing itself, scripting delicious little details that some folks might recognize as ironic but find too on-the-nose to be funny.

Starts with an avowed proponent of transparency waging a vicious campaign against "leakers" and truth-tellers, culminating with his unrighteous handling of Edward Snowden. Same guy assumes more Executive Power than all the Bushes combined. Wins the Nobel Peace Prize and proceeds to authorize extra-judicial murders of American citizens on foreign soil, conducted, mainly, by brave men and women wielding joysticks in a remote basement, just like in the video game version.

The Country That Satirized Itself then elects a person who is himself a kind of satire of the American Dream. He proceeds to nominate for his cabinet the single worst candidate for each job. The climate denier for the EPA. The foe of public education for Education. The CEO of the global oil company for Secretary of State. Who also has a weird relationship with an Evil Russian Dictator.

It's all too fulsome and juicy for any writer to outscript. And so we humbly step back from prognosticating and simply observe with wonder.

Having endured one war-maker after another throughout our voting lifetime, we're more inclined than ever to agree with John Lennon's assessment of the people controlling our world, the ones with the power to obliterate us all. He thought they were mad. Insane. Inmates running the asylum — a trope that's always made for great satire.

Greed is why we educate the masses just well enough that they behave, but not well enough that they might all transform themselves into high achievers.

- The Termite Squad

No Such Thing

I want to have high ideals
I want to love mankind
Trust my fellow man
Be loving, true and kind
But everyone tells me, "No!"
My parents tell me, "No!"
My teachers tell me, "No!"
Everyone tells me, "No such thing!"

There's no such thing as happiness
No such thing as love.
Life's a useless struggle; you better give it up.
No such thing as caring, no such thing as joy.
No such thing as equality;
you're so naive, young boy.

I want to change for better,
I want to live my life,
Help eliminate violence, hate, and strife,
But everyone tells me, "No!"
My parents tell me, "No!"
My teachers tell me, "No!"
Everyone tells me, "No such thing!"

There's no such thing as happiness,
No such thing as love.
Life's a useless struggle; you better give it up.

No such thing as caring, no such thing as joy.
No such thing as equality;
you're so naive, young boy.

I want to have high ideals,
I want to love mankind
Trust my fellow man,
Be loving, true and kind
But everyone tells me, "No!"
My parents tell me, "No!"
My teachers tell me, "No!"
Everyone tells me, "No such thing!"

Let's show 'em they're wrong.

-- The Clitboys, 1983

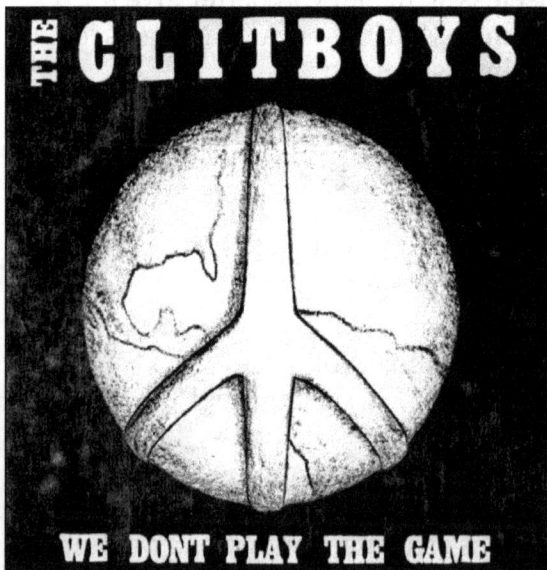

THE CLITBOYS

WE DONT PLAY THE GAME

The Day After the Revolution

. . . and to conclude, the Truth and Reconciliation Commission makes the following findings and recommendations.

+ Capitalism has been an interesting experiment which has now ended. We must identify a better organizing principle than greed.

+ Those who have aspired to the crimes of the 1% — hoarding wealth — but never managed to acquire their first billion are not innocent; they are merely less successful criminals.

+ Slavery is hereby abolished. Let it be recorded that for the first time in human history all of humankind has been completely emancipated.

+ Drug prohibition is hereby abolished; a national apology shall be given to those incarcerated for drug "crimes."

+ Prisons will be reserved solely for the incorrigibly violent, not as places to punish the non-violent.

+ There is a no shortage of anything, except kindness and compassion. All crises are matters of poor distribution.

+ The Gross Domestic Product metric shall be replaced by a National Happiness and Contentment Index.

+ War has ended. Love making has begun.

My Great Idea

Before I came along, the ongoing success of the Termite Squad was built on one key assumption: Old ladies can get away with more than the average person.

Ladies in general, of course. But, especially, *old* ladies. One-hundred years or more. Centenarians. *Centurions*, as the kids say.

Have you ever met a woman born in 2000, or earlier? They like to complain. Even though life expectancy is around, like, what, 104 these days? Her lost looks, her reduced pension, her ruinous healthcare costs. And she'll remind you repeatedly about how she didn't have to desalinate everything back in the day, how water used to be free and you didn't need a wind-gathering license.

Not hating on them. Old ladies are permitted to deliver soliloquies, because they're totally entitled to. Just like they're entitled to cut in line.

They do what they want. Very few of us complain. Of course we don't! They're *old*. They're adorable. The rudeness is sort of cute in a way, like a puppy. We understand.

How the Revolution Started:
Essays and Impertinent Thoughts

No one likes to say "no" to the elderly, to a frail and wizened woman who looks like your mother. No one wants to disappoint her mother.

When an old lady asks for help, she usually gets help. When an old lady asks for a little favor, some special treatment, she usually gets special treatment. Even when she's wearing an Endvest™.

My great idea was a simple idea: Keep the ladies, add the sexy.

Those were my exact words. That's exactly what I said to the Director of Operations, when they brought me in to make my pitch. I had cashed in all my banked favors and got the meeting, the face2face kind, right there in Langley. I knew I had only a few minutes to get their attention and hold it.

"Keep the ladies, add the sexy," I said, smiling my best *"I'm just a sassy little girl with a lot of moxie"* smile. It worked.

There were perfectly good reasons at first to restrict the Termite Squad to Centurions, to women 100 or more years-old. The most obvious being that they really could die any day. Plus, everyone involved in national security knew that the Elders strategy would be detected and defeated eventually. Argentina had already started denying entry visas to foreign senior citizens with mobility issues, and chatter in the diplomatic community suggested that Malaysia and Turkey were considering similar "anti-cripple" legislation. So now Termite Squad recruiters were looking for high-mobility Centurions – ladies who didn't need a chair. But, still, the bad guys were starting to put their guard up. They were on the lookout for shriveled Super Seniors.

It occurred to me the day I got my diagnosis: Why do you have to be old to be a hero? Why can't you be a hero when you're young and vivacious and you still have your figure?

Keep the ladies, add the sexy. I'm 28, OK? I don't look like the usual Termite.

I have above-average Liker stats. Above-average WorthScore©. Not bragging, but thanks to a fairly extensive network of personal feeds, my profile has been shared on the Home Page of some very important sites. #justbeingreal

I dated Ladante Mook (briefly) and Garreth Sparks (slightly longer), and that's not to mention some of my fleeting hook-ups, which I'm sure you're already checking. Search away. I'm not one to kiss and post. But at this point...I guess I can reveal that I had one (dreamy) night with Harry Spenser – and no, I'm not kidding. Check your arm. Put in our two names + Mumbai. You'll see. And yes, it was everything you would imagine it would be. Like one of his movies, but real. #delicious.

Eventually, I connected with the man of my dreams, my JJ, and those boys became nothing to me but fond memories. But I wouldn't trade them.

The point is looks matter. Right? Youth matters. I didn't make the rules. I just play by them.

So I impressed upon the Director that a potential Termite's ability to *gain access* was what made her valuable. The more access to powerful people the better. I told him, "Not many people can say 'no' to a sweet old lady. Even fewer can say 'no' to a sweet young one."

The Termite Squad's Director of Operations, who was officially separated from his wife when I met him, totally got my message. Or got me. Or both. But he got it.

I hope you do, too. I hope you understand.

We're all going to die. Some of us are just meant to be an attractive corpse.

I'm kidding but I'm not. You know what I mean?

I didn't plan my life out wanting to die young. I didn't want to be a martyr. No matter how expertly you've calibrated your algo-chip, sometimes life decides certain things for you. It's out of your hands. When that happens, you just have to make the best of it.

For me, it was an easy decision. When I got the diagnosis, it was a very easy decision. I wanted to be a member of the Termite Squad.

****

The Revolution Continues...

TheTermiteSquad.com

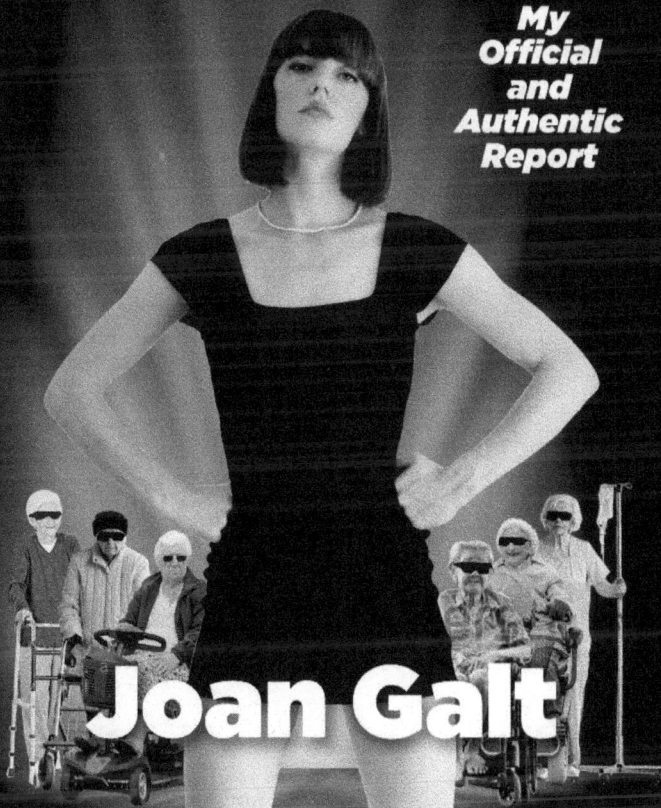

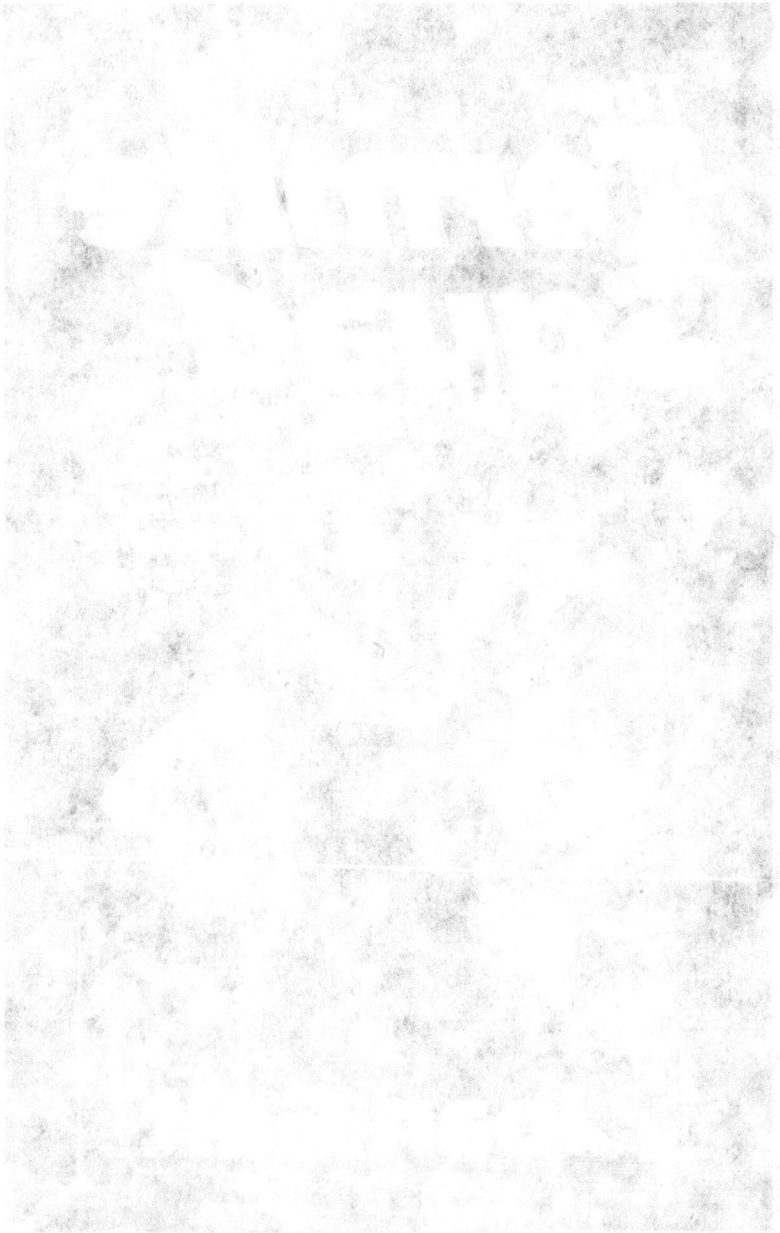

"A fascinating and strangely realistic near future, drawing the reader in with surprising and imaginative features."
— RANDOM HOUSE

"The structure of the book is fun, fast moving, brave, and perfect for the story."
— SIMON & SCHUSTER

"A well rendered projection of what would happen if today's techno-libertarians ever really had the chance to instill their values into society. Chilling and provocative."
— LITTLE BROWN

JOAN GALT

Official and Authentic Report

Presented by

Termite Squad Truth Association

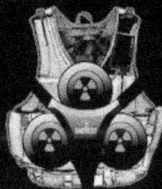

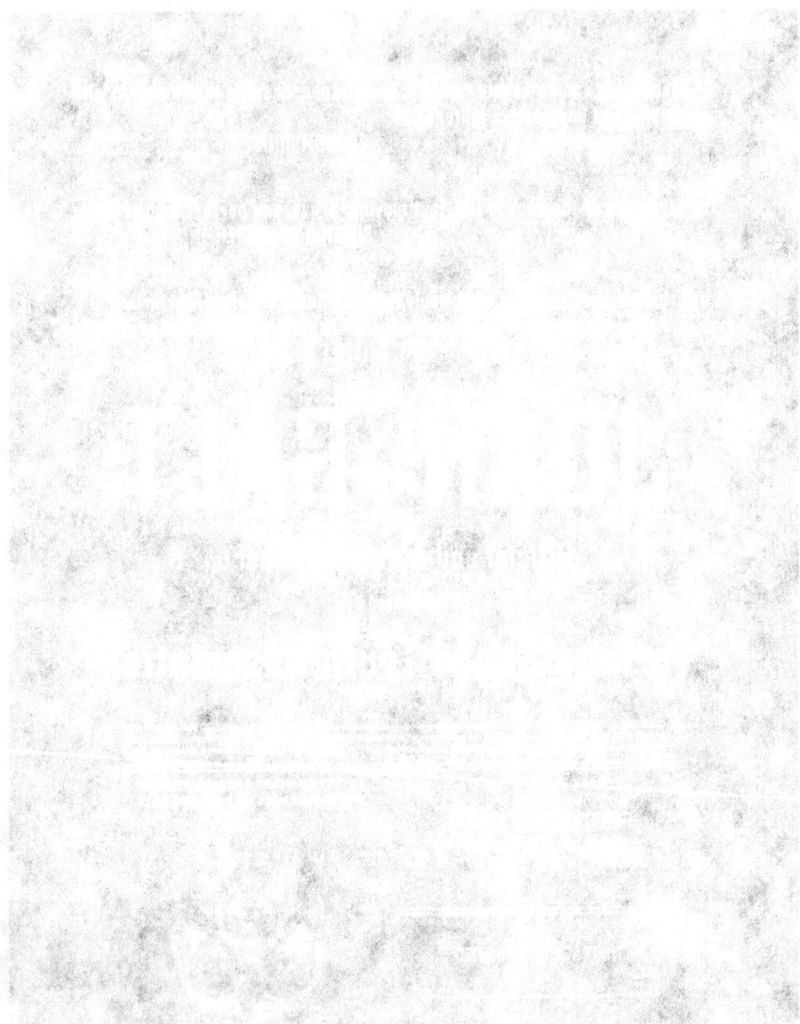

The author thanks the visionary team at Eggy Press for their tireless support of his creative efforts. Thanks, also, to Uwe Stender, literary agent, for passionately promoting essays and ideas that are difficult to sell. And thank you to the legions of editors, readers and writers whose community of mindfulness have inspired this work.

www.ingramcontent.com/pod-product-compliance
Lightning Source LLC
Chambersburg PA
CBHW050540280326
41933CB00011B/1655